Contents

People in the story

Ken Harada: a photographer
Sachiko: Ken's wife
Tetsuro: Ken's son
Kenzaburo Yoshimoto: the boss of Tokai Photo Agency
Takahanada: a famous sumo star
Kumiko Okada: Takahanada's girlfriend
Hiromitsu Shioiri: a Yakuza gunman
Fat man: works for Hiromitsu Shioiri
Chief Inspector Uchikawa of the Tokyo Police

Places in the story

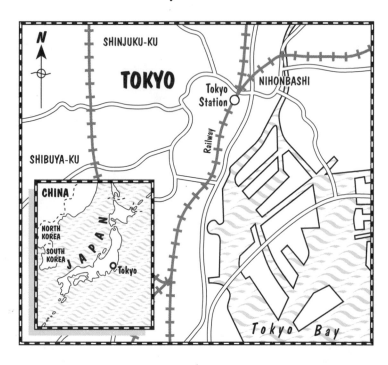

Chapter 1 *A photo*

It started with a telephone call. Just like any other day.

I'm Kenji, Kenji Harada. Everyone calls me Ken. I take photos. It's my job. I take photos for newspapers, for anybody who wants to buy them. I take photos of famous people. I have a Nikon camera and a darkroom in my flat. Sometimes work is good, sometimes it's bad.

Like I said, every day starts with a telephone call from Tokai Photo Agency. They buy my photos and sell them around the world. Sometimes they give me a lot of money for my photos, but sometimes they give me very little.

It was Thursday, 8.30 in the morning. Work was bad. It was often bad in January, February and March. It was April now, but it was also bad. My wife wasn't happy. She wanted money. She always wanted money.

I answered the telephone. It was the boss of Tokai Photo Agency. His name's Kenzaburo Yoshimoto. It's a big name for a small man. A very small man.

'Go to the Tokyo Garden Hotel at 10.30,' Yoshimoto said. He never said 'good morning' and he never said 'please'.

'Takahanada is going to the Tokyo Garden Hotel with his new girlfriend,' Yoshimoto said.

Takahanada! He was a famous sumo star in Japan.

'And be quick,' Yoshimoto said. 'Every photographer in Tokyo is going to be there.'

Takahanada was very good-looking and very rich, and

5

his new girlfriend, Kumiko Okada, was a beautiful actress. People said Takahanada wanted her to be his wife. Wow! I could sell a good photo of them for millions of yen. I dressed quickly, putting on my new black suit. I took my camera. I didn't have time for breakfast. I thought about the money.

Twenty minutes later I was on the streets of Tokyo. There was a lot of noise and there were a lot of people. I love Tokyo. It's a very beautiful city and it's mine!

I took a taxi. I didn't have much money, but I didn't want to be late. At 9.45 I was at the Tokyo Garden Hotel in Shinjuku. Shinjuku has a lot of expensive hotels and restaurants. There were about twenty-five photographers near the hotel.

'Hey, move!' said one photographer to another photographer, and then pushed him. Everyone wanted to get the photograph. Everyone wanted to be near Takahanada and the beautiful Kumiko Okada. Every photographer had an expensive camera and a very big lens. I saw my friend, Jun. He was a photographer too.

'Hey, Jun!' I called. 'They're coming in this door, right?'

'Sure,' called Jun, smiling.

I looked around. Where could I wait? I didn't know. There were a lot of photographers by the door of the hotel. It wasn't easy to take a good photograph from there. I walked down the street and looked around.

Next to the hotel was a coffee shop. I looked in the window. It looked nice, with white tables and flowers, and I was hungry and thirsty – I wanted a coffee and some breakfast.

A taxi stopped at the coffee shop. It was just a Tokyo

taxi, but then I saw them. Takahanada and Kumiko Okada! They got out of the taxi and went to the door of the coffee shop. From the coffee shop, you could get into the hotel.

I quickly took my camera and my big lens, and looked at them. I moved the lens so that I could see their faces. I could only see their faces.

Takahanada smiled at Kumiko and I took the photo. It was a very, very good photo. And it was mine, just mine.

Takahanada and Kumiko went into the hotel. I looked around. There were no photographers, just me. I walked quickly away from the hotel and called a taxi. I smiled. I had the only photo of Takahanada and Kumiko Okada. I was rich.

I was very happy. But I almost died because of that photo.

Chapter 2 *Help!*

I got into the taxi. The taxi driver looked at me. I could just see his eyes.

'Nihonbashi, please,' I said to him.

I wanted to go to my flat. I wanted to call Tokai Photo Agency. I wanted to tell Yoshimoto that I had a very good photo. The only photo of Takahanada and Kumiko Okada.

Then I heard the noise of a fast car. I looked across the street. Next to my taxi was another taxi, and in it was a man in a black suit. He looked at me. I smiled at him, but he didn't smile at me. Then I saw something in his hand. It was a gun.

'Aagh!' I said. I put my head down, under the window.

'What?' asked the taxi driver.

'Drive!' I said. 'That man's got a gun. He wants to kill me.'

The taxi driver looked over and saw the man with the gun. The taxi driver started to go very fast. I sat in the back of the taxi with my head down.

Ten minutes later we got to my flat.

'Is he there?' I asked the taxi driver.

'No,' he said. 'You're OK.'

I gave the taxi driver some money and got out of the taxi. I went into my flat quickly, and took the film out of my camera. Then I looked out of the window. I couldn't see the man with the gun. I couldn't see anybody.

I had the film in my hand. I wanted to take it to my darkroom, where I make my photos. I wanted to see my photo, the photo that was going to make me rich. But just then I heard the telephone. It was Sachiko, my wife. She wasn't happy.

'Ken, I must speak to you about Tetsuro,' she said. Tetsuro was our son; he lived with Sachiko and I saw him at weekends.

'What is it?' I asked. 'Isn't he well?'

'He's OK. But I need money for his new school things. You must come here – I must speak to you.'

Sachiko was never happy with me. I didn't have much work and I didn't have any money. And now it was April. An expensive time.

'OK,' I said. 'I'll come now. I've got something good to tell you.' My wife's flat was quite near to mine, just a kilometre away.

I looked out of my window again. I couldn't see anybody. I put on my jacket and took the film. I wanted to have that photo with me. I left the flat and soon I was at Sachiko's house.

Sachiko gave me green tea and biscuits. I asked her about Tetsuro's new school things.

'Ken,' she said, 'you must give me some money.'

I told her about the photograph. 'I'm going to be rich now,' I said. 'Just wait and see. This photo is going to make me rich.'

Sachiko smiled. 'Maybe,' she said.

I was always sad when I saw Sachiko. You see, I loved her. But did she love me? I didn't know. Sachiko didn't like Tokyo. She wanted to live somewhere nice, 'in the country' she said. But I couldn't find work in the country. Now Sachiko and I didn't live in the same flat. It wasn't easy. But I loved her.

An hour later, I went back to my flat. I went up to the door. But I didn't need the key. The door was open. I walked into my flat. Wow! The windows were broken; everything in my flat was broken.

I went into my darkroom, the room where I make my photos. Everything in there was broken too. There were films, water, photos, everything all over the floor. My beautiful darkroom!

I didn't feel well. I sat down. 'Somebody's looking for something,' I thought, 'and I think I know what it is.'

Chapter 3 *The key*

I was afraid. I telephoned the police. Two policemen came to my flat. One was tall, the other was short.

'Do you know who did this?' asked the tall one.

'No,' I said. 'But this morning I saw a man with a gun in a taxi.'

'Hmm,' said the short one. 'I see.'

The two policemen said 'hmm' a lot. Then they said goodbye.

'But I think he'll come back,' I said. 'Maybe next time he'll kill me!'

'Hmm,' said the short policeman. 'We'll call you later, but you must get a new door.' And then they left.

I sat down and looked at my flat. I started to put everything back in its place. It took a long time. A very long time. Then I went into my darkroom and took out my film. 'Now,' I said, 'now I can see my photo.'

I heard the telephone. I left the film in the darkroom and went to answer the telephone.

It was Yoshimoto. 'Go to Shibuya to take more sumo star photos. 4.30.'

'But . . .' I said. But Yoshimoto put the telephone down. Why did nobody listen to me? I looked at my watch. It was 3.30.

I found an envelope and went into my darkroom. I put the film in the envelope and put it in my jacket. I didn't want to lose this film. I didn't want anyone to take it. I took my camera and left my flat.

In the street I looked around. I couldn't see the man with the gun. I walked quickly to the station and took the train to Tokyo Station.

At the station I went to Left Luggage. I took a key. I looked at the key. It had a number on it. Number 93. I took the envelope with the film out of my jacket, and put it in locker 93. Then I took the number off the key and put it in the rubbish bin. I put the key in my jacket. 'Number 93,' I said.

It was 4.10 and I had to be at Shibuya at 4.30. I went out of the station to get a taxi. But a car stopped next to

me on the street. The driver quickly got out of the car and pushed me into the back. In the back of the car there was a big fat man, with dark glasses.

'Hey, what are you doing?' I asked. The car started.

The fat man next to me put his hand on my mouth.

'Any noise and you'll be sorry,' he said. The fat man took my camera and opened it.

'Hey!' I said. 'What . . .'

'No noise!' the man said. He took the new film out of the camera. 'This is a new film!' he said.

Then the fat man put something over my eyes and I couldn't see anything. We drove for about an hour.

The car stopped and the fat man pushed me out. I didn't know where I was. I couldn't hear the city. Now I was very afraid.

'You're not going to kill me, are you?' I asked.

The fat man said, 'No noise, OK?'

He pushed me into a house. It was cold. Then the fat man looked in my jacket.

'Where is the film?' he asked.

'What film?' I asked.

'Ah!' he said. 'What's this?' He found the key. The key for the locker at Tokyo Station. I didn't speak. Then he smiled.

'I know what this is,' he said. 'It's a key for a Left Luggage locker. Tell me the train station and locker number now, or you're dead.'

'It's Shibuya Station. Number 42,' I said.

The fat man put something over my mouth. I couldn't speak. He tied my arms to the chair with ropes. I couldn't move. Then he left me.

Chapter 4 *Run!*

It was just like a darkroom. There was no noise. I couldn't see and I couldn't move. I was afraid. I waited. Minutes, hours. I didn't know how long I was there.

I slept for a short time. When I slept I had a dream. In my dream I could see my teacher at the Tokyo School of Photography. His name was Mori-sensei. Mori-sensei spoke to me. Just like he did when I was a student.

'Harada-san,' Mori-sensei said to me, 'with the lens of the camera you can never see everything. When you take a photograph you *choose* what you want to see. Maybe there's

something you don't see. Maybe you don't see something important.'

It was cold. I thought about my son, Tetsuro. I didn't want to die. I wanted to move my hands but I couldn't.

Then I heard a noise. The door opened and someone came in.

'Come on. Make any noise and I'll kill you, OK?' It was the big fat man.

He took the things off my eyes and mouth. He started to take the ropes off. I knew it was now or never. He was fat; he couldn't run. I was afraid, but I knew it was now or never.

I pushed the fat man. He was big but he went back just like a tree. I saw my camera. I took it and ran quickly out of the house. It was dark and I didn't know where I was. I just started running into some trees. Then I heard a gun and the fat man saying, 'Come back, come back or I'll kill you!'

Then I heard someone very near me. I ran very fast. I didn't look back. I ran and ran. Now I couldn't hear the gun. I couldn't hear the man behind me. In front of me I saw a road. I ran to it.

I walked down the road. It was night and I was very tired. There weren't many cars. I wanted to stop them. I

needed help. I wanted to get back to Tokyo. I waved my arms and said, 'Stop! Stop!' but nobody stopped. They looked at me but they didn't stop.

Then, after about half an hour, a big lorry came down the road. I waved my arms and said, 'Stop! Stop!' The driver stopped. He smiled at me.

'Please,' I said, 'can you take me to the centre of Tokyo?'

'Get in,' said the lorry driver. 'I can take you near the centre.'

The driver started to ask me questions. But I was very tired and I slept. Half an hour later we stopped at a restaurant near the road. We were about eight kilometres from the centre of Tokyo.

'You must get out here,' said the lorry driver. 'Maybe you can get a taxi.'

I went into the restaurant and telephoned for a taxi. Then I waited for the taxi to come. I read a newspaper. On the front it said: *Yakuza gang man Toru Sato killed in Tokyo street.*

'Aagh!' I said. The Yakuza were very dangerous, like the Mafia.

I read the newspaper. They thought that a gang killed Toru Sato on a street in Shinjuku. It was the street where I took the photograph of Takahanada and Kumiko Okada. I thought about Mori-sensei, my teacher. 'You can't see everything,' he said.

The taxi came. I put the newspaper under my arm and left the restaurant quickly.

'Where do you want to go?' asked the driver.

'Tokyo Central Police Station,' I said. 'And fast!'

Chapter 5   *The police*

'Somebody wants to kill me!' I said to Chief Inspector Uchikawa of the Tokyo Police.

Uchikawa wore glasses, but he didn't look at me with his glasses. He looked at me over them.

'Please sit down, Mr Harada,' he said. I sat down. 'Now, why do you think someone wants to kill you?' he asked.

'Listen,' I said. 'You must come with me to Tokyo Station now. You and some of your men.'

I told him everything quickly. About the man with the gun in the taxi. About my flat and the broken doors and windows. About the fat man and the ropes and the blindfold.

'Hmm,' the Chief Inspector said.

'And I'm sure they want my photo,' I said.

'What photo?' the Chief Inspector asked.

'My photo of Takahanada and Kumiko Okada,' I said. I told him about the photo and about the film in the Left Luggage locker.

'Well, let's have a look at this photo,' said the Chief Inspector. I smiled.

'But we can do it tomorrow,' he said. 'It's too late now.'

'Listen!' I said. 'You don't understand! They have the key! I told them the wrong station, but they're going to go to Tokyo Station after that. They're going to find the film. Please come now!'

He looked at me over his glasses. 'Please,' I said.

Then the Chief Inspector understood. He called three of his men and we ran out of the door. I looked at the three policemen. They were very small. The Chief Inspector looked at me.

'These are good men,' he said. 'Wait and see.'

We got into a police car and drove quickly to Tokyo Station. Five minutes later we were at the station. We went to Left Luggage. Then we stopped.

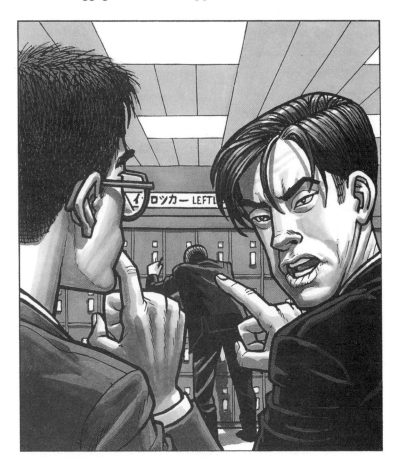

'Shh . . .' said the Chief Inspector.

There was a man there. A man in a black suit. He couldn't see us. I couldn't see his face, but I knew it was the man with the gun in the taxi.

'Chief Inspector,' I said, 'that's the man with the gun.'

'Shh!' said the Chief Inspector.

The man in the black suit was putting a key in all the lockers. There were three hundred lockers. We waited. Now he was at locker number 91. Then the Chief Inspector said 'Now!' to his men and the three men ran out. They were small but they were very fast. They pushed the man onto the floor. One of the policemen took the key and gave it to me.

The Chief Inspector went to the man. 'Get up!' he said. Uchikawa put his face very near the man's face. 'Well, well, Hiromitsu Shioiri,' he said. He looked at the man over his glasses and smiled. 'Now I have you. And this time you are going to prison for a very long time!'

'For what, Chief Inspector?' asked the man.

'For killing Toru Sato,' said Uchikawa.

'Ha!' The man smiled now. 'And how,' he asked, 'do you know that I killed Toru Sato? How?'

'I think it's time,' said the Chief Inspector, turning to me, 'for us to have a look at that photo.'

I looked at Shioiri's face but it didn't move. I opened locker number 93 and took out the envelope.

We got into the police car and drove to my flat. I looked at Shioiri again. Nothing. When we got to my flat, Shioiri and the three policemen waited. The Chief Inspector and I went into the darkroom.

'Just watch,' I said.

I took the film and opened it. Slowly, slowly, we started to see the photo of Takahanada and Kumiko Okada.

There was the big face of Takahanada looking at the beautiful Kumiko. They were very happy. It was a very, very good photograph. First, we saw the two stars, then slowly, slowly we could see the street behind them. The people walking, the restaurants and the shops. Then, yes – there he was, Hiromitsu Shioiri, the man who was now in my flat with the three policemen. It was him! And he had a knife in his hand.

And then in front of Shioiri, I saw a man. He was on his back in the street. It was Toru Sato. He was dead.

Chapter 6 *The country*

Chief Inspector Uchikawa was very happy.

'Thank you,' he said, smiling. 'Now Shioiri is in prison for twenty-five years. Because of your photo.'

Then there was the photo of Takahanada and Kumiko Okada. The photo that started it all. I sold the photo to Yoshimoto for sixty million yen.

Now I live in the country. With Sachiko and Tetsuro, my son. Like I said, I love Sachiko. 'Live with me again,' I said to her. 'We can go to the country.'

'Yes,' she said. 'I love you, but you didn't see it.'

So we live in the country. I love Tokyo but I love Sachiko more. We have a big house and we love it here. We are all very happy.

And my camera? I didn't take my camera to the country. I didn't want to take photos. It's too dangerous.

Mori-sensei was right. You can't see everything. 'Maybe there's something you don't see,' he said. 'Maybe you don't see something important.'

But sometimes the important thing is right there in front of you.

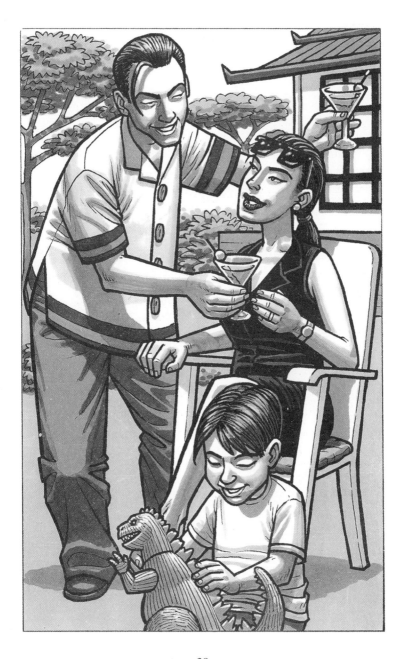

29

Cambridge English Readers

Other titles available at Levels 1 and 2:

Level 1

Help! *by Philip Prowse*
Frank Wormold is a writer. To help him finish one of his stories he starts to use a computer. But the computer gives him more help than he wants. Then he really needs 'help'!

Just Like a Movie *by Sue Leather*
Brad Black goes to the movies every weekend with his girlfriend, Gina. They are happy, but have no money. Then Brad has an idea and thinks that real life can be just like a movie – and that's when things go wrong.

John Doe *by Antoinette Moses*
The man they call John Doe lies in a hospital bed. The doctor wants to know who he is. But John Doe doesn't answer his questions. When John Doe leaves the hospital, the doctor finds out more about him than just his real name.

Level 2

Superbird *by Brian Tomlinson*

A spaceship crashes on a strange planet and everyone on it dies – except for Mary Mount. She helps the people of the planet to build their own spaceship and then returns home in it. But when she is back home, the trouble really begins.

The Double Bass Mystery
by Jeremy Harmer

Penny Wade is a musician. She goes to Barcelona with her orchestra to play. But her double bass is lost and then someone in the orchestra dies. The police want to know what happened and Penny's life changes as she learns the truth.

A Picture to Remember
by Sarah Scott-Malden

Cristina Rinaldi works for an art museum in Buenos Aires. One day she has a motorbike accident and can't remember some things. But there are two men who think she remembers too much, and they want to kill her before she can tell the police what she saw.

31

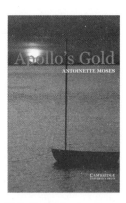

Apollo's Gold *by Antoinette Moses*

Liz studies and teaches archaeology in Athens. She goes on holiday to the beautiful and peaceful island of Sifnos. But the peace does not last long: a mysterious yacht arrives, one of the local men dies, and Liz becomes involved with some very dangerous people.

Jojo *by Antoinette Moses*

'There aren't any more days. There's just time. Time when it's dark and time when it's light. Everything is dead, so why not days too?' Everyone in Jojo's village is dead, and ten-year-old Jojo is alone.

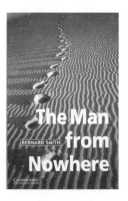

The Man from Nowhere
by Bernard Smith

A man is walking slowly in the desert. He is not wearing a shirt. The sun is on his back, which is burnt red. He cannot see, he cannot think. He does not know where he is or who he is. He only knows that he must keep moving. Keep moving, or die.

Logan's Choice
by Richard MacAndrew

'I'm Inspector Logan of the Edinburgh police,' Jenny said. 'I'm very sorry about the death of your husband.' Who killed Alex Maclennan? His friend, his wife or his wife's brother? It isn't easy but Inspector Logan has to choose.